Do You Know What Time It Is?

Seed Learning

Do you know what time it is?

Yes. It's 7 o'clock.

It's time to wake up.

Do you know what time it is?

Yes. It's 9 o'clock.

It's time
to go to school.

Do you know what time it is?

Yes. It's 12 o'clock.

It's time to eat lunch.

Do you know what time it is?

Yes. It's 6 o'clock.

It's time to go home.

Do you know what time it is?

Yes. It's 8 o'clock.

It's time to eat dinner.

Do you know what time it is?

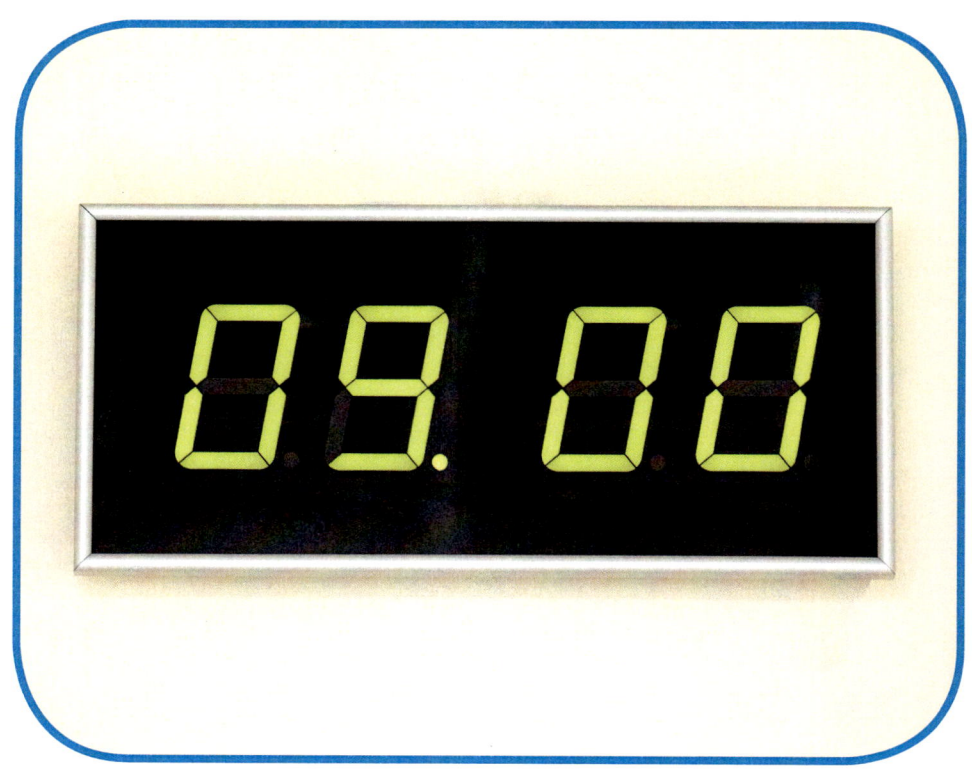

Yes. It's 9 o'clock.

It's time
to take a bath.

Do you know what time it is?

Yes. It's 10 o'clock.

It's time
to go to bed.

Let's learn about New Year's Day.

January

Sunday	Monday	Tuesday	Wednesday	Thursday	Friday	Saturday
					1	2
3	4	5	6	7	8	9
10	11	12	13	14	15	16
17	18	19	20	21	22	23
24	25	26	27	28	29	30

Trace the word January
and circle the date.